Architecture

Cool Women Who Design Structures

D1221570

Elizabeth
Schmermund

Illustrated by
Lena Chandhok

This book was manufactured by CGB Printers,
North Mankato, Minnesota, United States
August 2017, Job #228802

ISBN Softcover: 978-1-61930-546-5
ISBN Hardcover: 978-1-61930-542-7

Educational Consultant, Marla Conn

Questions regarding the ordering of this book should be addressed to
Nomad Press
2456 Christian St.
White River Junction, VT 05001
www.nomadpress.net

Printed in the United States.

~ Titles in the Girls in Science Series ~

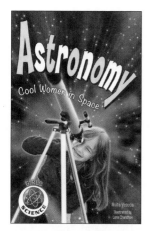

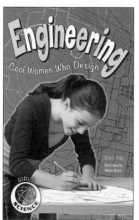

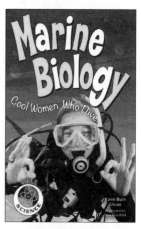

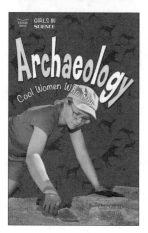

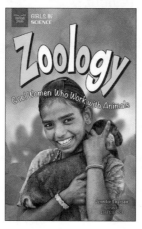

Check out more titles at www.nomadpress.net

How to Use This Book

In this book you'll find a few different ways to explore the topic of women in architecture.

The essential questions in each Ask & Answer box encourage you to think further. You probably won't find the answers to these questions in the text, and sometimes there are no right or wrong answers! Instead, these questions are here to help you think more deeply about what you're reading and how the material connects to your own life.

There's a lot of new vocabulary in this book! Can you figure out a word's meaning from the paragraph? Look in the glossary in the back of the book to find the definitions of words you don't know.

Are you interested in what women have to say about architecture? You'll find quotes from women who are professionals in the architecture field. You can learn a lot by listening to people who have worked hard to succeed!

Primary sources come from people who were eyewitnesses to events. They might write about the event, take pictures, or record the event for radio or video. Why are primary sources important?

PS

Interested in primary sources? Look for this icon.

Use a QR code reader app on your tablet or other device to find online primary sources. You can find a list of URLs on the Resources page. If the QR code doesn't work, try searching the Internet with the Keyword Prompts to find other helpful sources.

CONTENTS

INTRODUCTION
Building Our World

Look all around you. If you are sitting comfortably inside a school, a library, or your own home, you are enjoying the work of an architect. If you find yourself outside, the buildings around you— whether they are skyscrapers, cottages, shopping malls, or sports arenas—were all designed by architects. Architects build our world with the help of engineers and contractors, who bring the designs to life.

Architects spend long hours using their imaginations to create functional spaces in all kinds of buildings. They make these visions a reality using the laws of science. This means that architects need to use a lot of their skills at once, including those in math, science, and art.

Humans have been constructing buildings since the dawn of civilization. Why? Because our survival has depended on it.

The very first architects built small huts out of natural materials such as wood, mud, grass, and leaves. These buildings could mean the difference between life and death. If it was very cold outside or raining—or perhaps a predator was on the hunt—these buildings could protect early humans. Early architects made it possible for us to survive and develop into the species we are today.

Architects remain very important to all of our lives. Without them, we wouldn't have the safety or comfort of our homes. Contemporary architects need to construct buildings that are safe, that fulfill a certain function, and that look nice. Often, they also have to think about the cost of materials, their impact on the environment, and the project's timeline. Today's architects might specialize in building particular structures, such as homes, apartment buildings, or shopping malls.

The Earliest Architects

Archaeologists are scientists who study ancient history through artifacts. They agree that humans first developed simple buildings around 30,000 years ago. During this time, people lived as hunter-gatherers, which means they roamed the land in search of food and rarely stayed in one spot.

The earliest structures were simple tents that hunter-gatherers could easily build and then take down before moving to the next spot. These were most likely constructed by leaning branches together or against trees and then covering them with branches and leaves to protect against rain or snow.

As human beings gradually settled down and gave up the nomadic lifestyle, they began to build more permanent structures. These early settlements—constructed by some of the earliest architects—began to pop up around 8,000 years ago.

You can read about one important site of early human habitation, called Dolni Vêstonice, which is in the present-day Czech Republic. Look at pictures of the site. Can you spot the tents?

Dolni Vêstonice tent 🔍

In *Architecture: Cool Women Who Design Structures*, you will learn more about the history of architecture. You'll also meet three women who are working in architecture today and discover what they do.

Patricia Galván is a project architect who focuses on commercial buildings. She mentors other women in the field. Farida Abu-Bakare has begun her career in architecture with a specialty in laboratory design. And Maia Small has worked in a wide variety of fields in architecture, including teaching architecture to students, opening her own architectural firm, and working for the San Francisco Planning Department.

All of these women have taken different career paths in their chosen fields and have overcome many obstacles to get where they are today. Maybe their stories will inspire you! But, before we meet them, let's learn a bit more about the history of architecture and women's roles as architects.

66 Every architect is—necessarily—a great poet. **99**

—Frank Lloyd Wright,
architect

CHAPTER 1

A History of Architecture

What are some things that separate human beings from animals? For one, humans have developed advanced language to communicate. Equally important, we have also been able to build and to create. Our most important creations, especially in our early history, were functional and allowed us to survive against the odds. Before we even created art, humans designed simple structures to protect themselves against the elements.

The first buildings were basic tents that could easily be built up and taken down. When people began to turn to farming and settled down about 8,000 years ago, they created the first permanent buildings and villages and towns.

One of the earliest towns that we know of is called Jericho, which is located near the Jordan River in Palestine. Here, early architects built circular homes made of dried mud and straw.

These were small huts, typically with just one room and a hearth, an area to build a fire for cooking and heat. Gradually, 70 of these circular huts were built around Jericho. If you go visit the ancient town today, you can still see the foundations of some of these buildings. They have certainly stood the test of time!

As time went on, during thousands of years, different societies built up more towns like Jericho. The houses became more and more complex. People began to construct paved roads as these towns grew larger and larger. Just as importantly, these ancient architects built temples. These are structures in which people could worship their gods.

We do not fully understand the purpose of these temples or religious structures today. But we do know that structures were no longer just for protection—they were for spiritual guidance.

Stonehenge in Wiltshire, England

This marked an important turning point in both the history of architecture and in the history of human civilization.

The most famous of these early structures used for spiritual purposes is called Stonehenge. It looks like a ring of large rocks, with stones placed perpendicular to the standing stones to create archways.

Archaeologists believe that Stonehenge was built around 3000 BCE. That's more than 5,000 years ago! It might have been used for burials and religious ceremonies. Today, much of Stonehenge still stands—proof that these earliest architects used surprisingly advanced methods to ensure the stability of their structures.

Many other ancient monuments still stand today. We can visit them and marvel at how ancient architects—who did not have computers, modern tools, or a full understanding of physics—could build such impressive structures.

Perhaps the most awe-inspiring of these ancient structures are the pyramids of Egypt. First built around 2500 BCE, these pyramids were enormous burial structures for beloved rulers.

The largest, the Great Pyramid of Giza, stands nearly 500 feet tall and was built during a period of 20 years. For nearly 4,000 years, it was the tallest man-made structure in the world!

Archaeologists and historians still don't know exactly how ancient Egyptian architects, builders, and workers managed to create such a large and perfectly symmetrical structure. The ancient Egyptians only had tools made of softer metal and stone, ropes, and pulleys to help them build. They didn't have access to construction trucks or any kind of electrical equipment!

How in the world could they have built such large and perfect structures that would stand for thousands of years?

Ask & Answer

Why do you think the ancient Egyptians decided to construct pyramids, instead of another shape?

As you can see, by the time the pyramids were built in Egypt, architecture had completely changed. No longer were buildings small and simple. Now, great temples were being planned and created, requiring the use of teams of architects, builders, and laborers all working together.

The pyramids are another example of how the function of buildings had also changed. Far from Stonehenge, people were building for spiritual practices as well. The Egyptian pharaohs believed that if their bodies were kept safe in the pyramids, they would cross into another world upon their deaths.

THE GREEKS AND ROMANS

Without early architects, the ancient cities of Greece and Rome would not have been built. In particular, the architecture of ancient Greece became an important model for later civilizations. Even today, buildings are being built that are inspired by ancient Greek architecture.

Around the first century BCE, Greek architects developed their own architectural style. Greek architecture was later organized into three separate categories, or orders: the Doric, the Ionic, and the Corinthian. These orders are just different styles of architecture, with the Doric being the earliest and simplest design and the Corinthian being the most recent and most elaborate.

What the Greeks did with this formal structure was to show that different styles of architecture could have different functions.

Mathematical proportion and perspective was also an important part of Greek architecture. The Greeks wanted to model their architecture after the beauty of the natural world. They mimicked a special number, or ratio, called the golden mean. The golden mean is found in many living things.

The ancient Greeks understood that sometimes the human eye distorts what it sees. This can make something that is perfectly straight seem curved.

For this reason, ancient Greek architects calculated how human eyes would view the structures they built. They adjusted their structures to make them look perfectly straight even though they were not. These new architectural models became important for the Romans and for later civilizations as they modeled their own architecture on that of the Greeks.

While we might not know much about many individual architects in the ancient world, we do know about one—Marcus Vitruvius Pollio. Known as Vitruvius, he was born around 80 BCE.

All we know about the life of Vitruvius is that he lived in the Roman Empire. We know far more about his work, though, because his books survive even today.

The Golden Mean

The golden mean, also called the golden ratio, became a very important mathematical rule to follow in ancient Greek architecture. This number is approximately 1.618 and is found all around the natural world. The golden mean is the number you get if you take a line and divide it in two, so that the whole line divided by the longest part of the line is equal to the longest part of the line divided by the smallest part of the line. Sound complicated?

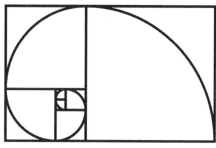

A visualization of the golden mean

We actually see the golden mean everywhere, from the way in which sunflower seeds grow to the proportions of spiral shells. The ancient Greeks thought that this number was the most beautiful and perfect proportion, which is why they used it in their buildings!

You can learn more about the golden mean, as well as how to calculate it, at the Math Is Fun website.

golden ratio ⌕

In particular, Vitruvius wrote an important book in Latin called *De Architectura*, which is known today as *The Ten Books on Architecture*. Vitruvius knew about and was inspired by Greek architecture. He wrote about the purposes and forms of this architecture. In fact, it was Vitruvius who first categorized Greek architecture into the three orders of Doric, Ionic, and Corinthian.

His book also stated that the point of architecture is to imitate nature by using natural materials to shield people from the elements.

Perhaps Vitruvius is best known for his statement that good architecture must have three qualities. It must be solid, it must be useful, and it must be beautiful. These rules became an important part of architecture. Many later architects followed Vitruvius in creating buildings that exhibited these properties.

66 Consequently, since such a wide discipline should be enriched, and overflow with many different kinds of expertise, I do not think that people can justifiably profess themselves architects at the drop of a hat. 99

—Vitruvius,
from *De Architectura*

RENAISSANCE ARCHITECTS

Later architects included Filippo Brunelleschi and Leon Battista Alberti. Brunelleschi was the first modern engineer and a founding father of the Renaissance. He lived between 1377 and 1446. Battista Alberti was an Italian Renaissance architect who lived from 1404 until 1472.

Filippo Brunelleschi was inspired by earlier Greek and Roman architects. He rediscovered a system of construction, called linear perspective, that was used by ancient architects but had been forgotten. Filippo Brunelleschi used these ancient techniques—as well as machines that he built himself—to complete some important architectural projects. These include the dome of the Cathedral of Santa Maria del Fiore, known as the Duomo, in Florence, Italy.

In turn, he went on to inspire another important architect, Leon Battista Alberti.

Throughout his lifetime, Leon Battista Alberti helped design many famous buildings, including Rucellai Palace in Florence, Italy. He also worked on several projects at the Vatican, which is the seat of the Catholic Church. Inspired by Vitruvius and Brunelleschi, he designed his buildings according to the three qualities of good architecture—solid, useful, and beautiful.

Battista Alberti elevated architecture to Renaissance ideals. He also wrote a treatise on architecture inspired by Vitruvius's *De Architectura*. Titled *De Re Aedificatoria*, or *On the Art of Building*, this was the first printed book on architecture when it came out in 1485. Because it brought greater attention to Vitruvius's work, *De Architectura* was published for the first time in 1486.

Linear Perspective

Linear perspective is a system that creates an illusion of depth when drawing on paper. While Greek and Roman artists had been using linear perspective for many years, this art technique was lost in the Middle Ages. Then, around 1420, Brunelleschi rediscovered this ancient technique. According to tradition, Brunelleschi studied ancient Greek and Roman art and was able to reconstruct how classical artists created depth in paintings. This was through the use of a vanishing point, or a point on the horizon of a piece of artwork where parallel lines (called orthogonals) drawn on the paper will meet. As an artist draws objects closer to the vanishing point, they become proportionally smaller and smaller. This gives the illusion of depth in the painting—and was the answer to how the ancient Greeks and Romans had created such convincingly real artwork!

His book remained the most important book on architecture until the eighteenth century. It was the first time someone had written an organized account of architecture as an art that was necessary for the well-being of people and the preservation of the government.

Drawing on the Greeks, he also showed that perfect harmony and proportion were necessary for architectural beauty and function. From that point on, architecture played a role of social importance— it was a science and an art form, and needed to be structurally perfect as well as beautiful.

As architecture gained importance in Renaissance society, beautiful and ornate buildings became symbols of power and wealth. From the fifteenth through the eighteenth century, architects designed important palaces throughout Europe.

One of the most magnificent of these constructions is the Palace of Versailles in France. The palace was originally designed by the famous French architect Louis Le Vau (1612–1670). Eventually, after being expanded during a period of more than 100 years, the palace itself reached a size of more than 700,000 square feet and contained more than 700 rooms and 67 staircases.

Today's average home size is approximately 2,500 square feet—more than 280 times smaller than Versailles! Historians believe that the palace cost the equivalent of more than $2 billion in today's money.

Palace of Versailles in France

This luxurious style grew somewhat outdated throughout the eighteenth and nineteenth centuries. But European architects continued to look at classical Latin and Greek architecture for inspiration throughout the 1800s.

There are different names for different movements in architectural style inspired from ancient Greece and ancient Rome. These include Baroque, the Palladian movement, Greek Revival, and Gothic. Architects who followed these popular styles, however, all turned toward the past for inspiration.

NEW ARCHITECTURAL FORMS

In the nineteenth century, architectural styles began to change even more. In European architecture, architects were exposed to different kinds of designs from Egypt and India, among other countries.

Architectural Styles

During certain historical periods, particular styles of building have become popular among top architects, who have reproduced them again and again in their works. These groupings of architectural styles make it easy to date certain constructions based on the architectural details used.

Gothic is a dramatic style of architecture used in cathedrals between the thirteenth through sixteenth centuries. Baroque, from the sixteenth century, represented both a return to Roman techniques and Catholic iconography. Palladian, used in the seventeenth and eighteenth centuries, was based on the work of architect Andrea Palladio (1508–1580). Greek Revival was used in Europe and the United States at the end of the eighteenth century and was modeled after ancient Greek architecture.

Explore many different architectural styles—including those from the ancient world—on this website.

architectural styles kids 🔍

They also learned to use different materials in construction. Some of these included materials such as iron and glass.

An important new movement in architecture, called Art Nouveau, began in the early 1900s. Art Nouveau is distinctive, which means it is easy to identify architecture that uses this style. This movement focused on mixing old styles of architecture with completely new forms.

Iron and glass were used often in Art Nouveau architecture, as was stylized, or exaggerated, designs. If you walk around the streets of Paris, France, today, you can still find many Art Nouveau structures. This style of architecture flourished in the "City of Lights" during the early 1900s.

Art Nouveau was the beginning of a more extreme change in the history of architecture—the development of Modernism. Modernist architects wanted to distinguish their works from past architectural works, rather than just copying or building upon them.

Ask & Answer

Today, some people around the world are designing tiny homes where people can live cheaply, sustainably, and simply. Would you ever live in a tiny home? Why or why not?

THE RISE OF MODERNISM

Modernism emerged as an artistic movement during and after the two world wars in the early- and mid-twentieth century. The movement was not just within architecture, but within painting, photography, and literature, among other domains.

World War I and World War II completely changed how people thought of the world. Artists and architects began looking for ways of describing their new reality through their artwork. Also, new technologies began to emerge that allowed builders to use new kinds of materials in their constructions.

Modernist architects wanted to do away with Greek- and Latin-inspired ornamentation. These elements had dominated architectural design for hundreds of years. Instead, architects wanted to build structures that would surprise people.

Famous modernist architects include Frank Lloyd Wright (1867–1959), Ludwig Mies van der Rohe (1886–1969), and Le Corbusier (1887–1965). They began to design buildings that followed certain patterns.

These patterns included simple designs that eliminated unnecessary detail or ornamentation. These designs used straight or curved lines and right angles and displayed the natural appearance of materials. They also featured large windows and flat roofs.

> 66 I am particularly fond of concrete, symbol of the construction progress of a whole century, submissive and strong as an elephant, monumental like stone, humble like brick. 99

—Carlos Villanueva,
architect

Typical construction materials for Modernist buildings included glass, steel, and reinforced concrete. These are notably strong and durable materials.

In America, Frank Lloyd Wright coined the term "form follows function," which became a motto of sorts for the movement. This means that the form, or shape, of a building should be determined by its purpose. Interestingly, this idea is rooted in the works of Vitruvius!

The concept of form following function was usually interpreted to mean that if a building was to be used as a school, for example, then there was no need for fancy molding, columns, or other ornamentation. The building should simply serve its purpose as a school.

Ask & Answer

Look around your home. Do you know who designed it and when? What are some things you like about the design of your home? What are some things you don't like?

Frank Lloyd Wright is famous for his contribution to modernist design. In his "organic architecture," buildings are in harmony with their natural surroundings. The building itself should include natural materials and be built as a natural whole.

Today, many architects are focused on sustainable architecture and using materials that do not harm our environment in the building process. These architects attempt to use biodegradable materials, or materials that will not eventually come to remain in landfills for many decades or even longer.

They try to use designs that include solar energy or even "green roofs," which are covered with plants. This was pioneered by Frank Lloyd Wright in the middle of the twentieth century in his philosophy of organic architecture.

ARCHITECTS TODAY

Earlier in the history of architecture, a finished building was viewed as the masterwork of a talented individual. Architects in the twenty-first century know the importance of teamwork and do not focus as much on individual work.

Different architects fulfill different roles on their teams, and they all work on their own special tasks to complete a project. Many architects need more than a knowledge of math, design, and drafting—also called architectural drawing.

Fallingwater

Frank Lloyd Wright designed a house that he called Fallingwater in the state of Pennsylvania. Today, this is known as the perfect example of organic architecture because of its use of flowing water both inside and outside the house. The natural surroundings of the house are built into its very design.

Visit the official Fallingwater website to learn more about Frank Lloyd Wright's most famous building. You can even plan a visit with a guided tour!

Fallingwater Frank Lloyd Wright 🔍

Fallingwater, designed by Frank Lloyd Wright

photo credit: Carol M. Highsmith's America, Library of Congress

Architects also need to know about sustainability and social behavior. This means that they work together to create a building, generally known as a "project," that will fulfill both the needs of the environment and the people who will use it. A notable example of contemporary architecture includes One World Trade Center in New York City. Known unofficially as the Freedom Tower, the building was designed to honor those who lost their lives on September 11, 2001, as well as to be a functional office building.

Architect Daniel Libeskind first proposed the design in 2002, but many team members helped to make this design a reality. The original design was changed before being finalized in 2005.

Freedom Tower is made up of steel, concrete, and blast-resistant glass. It reaches a height of 1,776 feet, a number that holds symbolic importance in the United States. The year 1776 is when the United States declared independence from Great Britain.

Ask & Answer

Think about your favorite building. It could be one you use every day or one you've seen only on television. Why is it your favorite? What do you like about it?

Freedom Tower is currently the fourth-tallest building in the world. David Childs, one of the architects working on the project, said, "The discourse about Freedom Tower has often been limited to the symbolic, formal, and aesthetic aspects, but we recognize that if this building doesn't function well, if people don't want to work and visit there, then we will have failed as architects."

This reflects a common belief among contemporary architects. A building should be nice to look at and it should, if necessary, hold symbolic meaning or reflect certain important values. However, it also needs to function well for the people who will be using the building every day.

WOMEN IN ARCHITECTURE

Looking back at the history of architecture, it is easy to see a history of great male architects. While women have always been involved in architecture, they have not always been recognized for their work.

Important early female architects who set the stage for female architects today include Louise Blanchard Bethune (1856–1913) and Josephine Wright Chapman (1867–1943). For many people, these names are not as well known as the names of famous male architects.

> 66 A city has to take the long view, the
> view for the common good. 99
>
> **—Amanda Burden,**
> architect and urban planner

More recently, Zaha Hadid (1950–2016) became one of the most influential and important architects in the world because of her work. Born in Iraq, Zaha went on to create her own architectural style that used many curves and fluid forms. These were said to imitate the continuity and chaos of modern life.

Zaha founded her own architectural firm in 1980 and created some of the world's most iconic structures. These include MAXXI, which is the National Museum of the 21st Century Arts in Rome, Italy, and the London Aquatics Centre for the 2012 Summer Olympics in London, England. She also designed the Contemporary Arts Center in Cincinnati, Ohio, as well as many other buildings.

In 2004, Zaha became the first woman to win the Pritzker Architecture Prize, the top architectural prize in the world. In 2008, she was listed as one of the world's most powerful women and, in 2010, she was named by *Time* magazine as one of the world's most influential thinkers. Zaha passed away in 2016, but her architectural design firm, Zaha Hadid Architects, which employs more than 400 people, continues to work on important projects.

Zaha Hadid is a shining example of how far women can go in the field of architecture, but there are still far fewer women than men in architecture today. Only 16 percent of members in the professional group American Institute of Architects are women.

While 42 percent of graduates today in architecture are women, only 25 percent of professional architects are women. However, the number of women working in architecture is growing every year.

Sophia Hayden Bennett

Sophia Hayden Bennett (1868–1953) was born in Santiago, Chile. In 1890, she became the first woman to receive a degree in architecture from the Massachusetts Institute of Technology (MIT). For the first year after her graduation, she tried to find a job working as an architect, but was unsuccessful. She gave up looking and turned to teaching technical drawing at a high school in Boston.

In 1891, Bennett heard about a call for female architects to submit designs for what was called the "Woman's Building," which would be featured in the World's Columbian Exhibit in Chicago, Illinois. She submitted a design based on her college thesis and won first prize. Men who had won a similar design competition were awarded $10,000 as their prize, but Bennett was awarded only $1,000.

STUDYING TO BE AN ARCHITECT

Are you a creative person? Do you like solving problems? Are you good at listening to other people? All of these qualities are important for an architect.

Architects combine art and science to build structures that are strong, beautiful, and functional. If you are thinking about becoming an architect, it's a good idea to take some art classes, where you'll learn about perspective and the different decorative forms.

The building was a success and Bennett received a gold medal for her design. However, she was often critiqued for creating too "feminine" a design. When Bennett did not attend the building's dedication ceremony in 1892, rumors spread that she had suffered a mental breakdown. Some male architects used these rumors as proof that women had no place in the field of architecture.

The Woman's Building was the last project Bennett ever designed. She died in 1953.

It's also a good idea to study hard in science classes. You'll learn about physics, gravity, forces, and loads.

The ability to listen to people is another important trait for an architect to have. When an architect begins to design a building, they need to listen to the people who will be using the building.

What do those people need the building for? What role is it supposed to accomplish? Does the building need to be energy efficient? What is the surrounding area like? How will the building blend into that environment?

Architects also need problem-solving skills. What happens when they encounter a problem with the design or construction? They need to be able to solve it without spending too much money or time!

Math, engineering, and language are good subjects to study if you're interested in architecture. Every architectural design relies on math and engineering to create a building that can stand, so a solid understanding of these concepts is critical. Language classes will help you to communicate with clients and other architects.

There are many amazing female architects working in the field right now. Three of these women—Patricia Galván, Farida Abu-Bakare, and Maia Small—share their stories with you in this book. Maybe their stories of hard work and passion will inspire you!

CHAPTER 2

Patricia Galván

On a typical day, you might find Patricia hard at work at her desk or on the phone with a client. Or, she might be at a construction site wearing a hard hat and holding architectural plans. These might sound like very different tasks for someone to take on, but not for a project architect such as Patricia. Her days are filled with many different tasks to accomplish, as she oversees the construction of buildings from early planning and drawings to their development on construction sites!

Patricia was born in Santa Clara, California. She was raised with a sister two years older than her. When Patricia was three years old, her parents divorced. She also has several half-siblings on her father's side.

Patricia's mother was a strong role model for both girls. Patricia's mom struggled early on in her own career, when her mom and dad encouraged her to focus on finding a husband and starting a family rather than choosing a career path. Although Patricia's mother wanted to go away to college, her parents insisted that she stay near home and complete a secretarial program. This was a training course where women learned to type and take dictation to prepare them for jobs as secretaries.

While Patricia's mother was working as a secretary for several large companies, she met Patricia's father. But, during their marriage, he became abusive. Patricia's mom battled for full custody to take care of her children, and eventually won. But she spent many years struggling to provide financially for her family, which was especially hard without a college degree.

Ask & Answer

Have you been in difficult situations with friends or family members? Do you feel as though these difficult times have made you stronger? Why?

> 66 Architecture is particularly difficult for women; there's no reason for it to be. 99
>
> **—Zaha Hadid,**
> architect

According to Patricia, "My mom did everything she could to make sure that my sister and I would not follow in her footsteps. I remember her picking me up from preschool and drilling us on [the years of schooling that] would follow . . . [all the way to] college!"

Patricia was lucky to have such a strong role model for a mother. She credits her mother's strength, work ethic, and passion for her children for helping Patricia become the woman she is today. Patricia says, "She did everything she could to expose us to opportunities for growth and advancement, but the decision was always ours to make. I always knew I had her support, no matter which career path I chose."

In fact, Patricia had already chosen her career path from a very young age—perhaps as young as three! She can vividly remember the floor plan of the home she lived in as a preschooler. She says, "I can't help but think that I was meant to be an architect."

Patricia began her more academic interest in architecture while attending a Catholic private school in Mountain View, California.

Do your parents pressure you to excel at school or in your hobbies? Even if it is sometimes frustrating, do you think their interest pushes you to do better?

Mountain View is a city in northern California near San Francisco. It is named after the beautiful Santa Clara Mountains that reach up over the city.

The high school Patricia attended was called Saint Francis High School. She was able to attend because she earned scholarships with her good grades. Patricia always enjoyed art classes in particular, and loved working on craft projects at her desk instead of going outside and playing sports.

One of the assignments that she remembers most from Saint Francis High School was given in a class on religion. Her religion teacher told Patricia to interview someone who worked in a career that she might want to pursue after high school. After the interview, she was expected to write a report about that person and their chosen career.

While Patricia wasn't able to interview an architect, she did get a chance to speak with a civil engineer. A civil engineer is someone who designs and builds structures such as bridges, roads, and tunnels.

What Do Civil Engineers Do?

Civil engineers work hard to find practical and creative solutions to large-scale problems. They build the structures that people use every day. For example, civil engineers plan and design transportation systems, such as the New York City subway system, which is one of the largest underground subway systems in the world. Their structures need to make sense for the people who use them while also following the laws of physics, meaning that the structures are safe and sturdy. Civil engineers also design bridges, canals, tunnels, and other important structures that people around the world rely on every day. If we didn't have civil engineers, we would live in a very different world!

A New York City Subway 6 train approaching
Parkchester station in the Bronx

photo credit: Robert McConnell

The civil engineer spoke passionately about his job. "I got the sense that his satisfaction came from more than just pride, but rather from being a part of a team that had successfully and beautifully accomplished their goal," Patricia says.

He didn't make it sound like the job was always easy. He told Patricia that there were many "roadblocks" along the way. But this only made completing a project even more gratifying in the end.

This opened Patricia's eyes to the way that architecture, too, could be both challenging and fulfilling. Patricia knew that by becoming an architect, she could "impact [her] community for the better."

While in high school, Patricia did very well in all of her classes. She had a full schedule, and also took on many different extracurricular activities. Patricia was a cheerleader and was also in the marching band, jazz band, and the symphonic band.

Being in these bands was her favorite part of high school, she says. "There was so much less pressure to be cool and to fit in," Patricia reflects. "We were all in the same boat—we were all band nerds together. Put us all in the same room with our instruments, and together we made beautiful music."

The pressure began mounting on Patricia during her junior year in high school. That year, she had to build an art portfolio for applications to architecture schools. It was hard to manage this while also keeping a full load of classes and extracurricular activities.

Patricia says that it would have been impossible without the help of her academic advisors and teachers. "Nobody ever told me I was crazy or that it couldn't be done in time," she recalls. "Nobody ever told me that they would not help me. I was so blessed!"

66 God created paper for the purpose of drawing architecture on it. Everything else is, at least for me, an abuse of paper. 99

—Alvar Aalto,
architect

THE NEXT STEP

Patricia's hard work soon paid off. She was accepted into the school of architecture at the University of Southern California in Los Angeles, California. This is an accredited architecture school, which means that it is recognized by professional architecture organizations. Attending an accredited school meant that Patricia would be able to take architecture and design courses in her very first year in college. She was excited to get started!

To go to school in Los Angeles, Patricia had to leave her home in northern California and move to the southern part of the state. She was far from home and her schoolwork was challenging. Patricia had been warned by many people that architecture school would be difficult. But, she says, when she looks back at her time in architecture school, she "can't help but chuckle," because college was much easier than embarking on a career!

At college, Patricia dove into design and architecture courses. She wanted to immerse herself in her major from the beginning of college. That way, she could decide if architecture was really her passion. If it wasn't, then she would pick another major and focus on planning for a different career.

Patricia soon realized that architecture was the only thing she wanted to pursue.

She loved taking design courses and learning how to draft. By the start of Patricia's senior year, she had also completed a study abroad program in Southeast Asia. While there, she was able to fulfill some of her major requirements during the summer. This meant that she had some free time in her schedule.

Patricia decided that she wanted to get a taste of what working in architecture was really like. Maybe, she thought, even though she liked taking courses in architecture, she wouldn't like working in the field. So Patricia took a semester off from college to work as a paid intern at a small architectural firm in Culver City, California. This experience only confirmed for Patricia that she had found her calling—and that she knew what she wanted to do for the rest of her life.

However, things do not always go according to plan. When Patricia graduated from college with her architecture degree, the rules for becoming a licensed architect had just been changed.

Becoming licensed means that you are officially recognized as an architect by a state or states. It means you can legally practice in your field.

66 Architecture is not an inspirational business, it's a rational procedure to do sensible and hopefully beautiful things; that's all. 99

—Harry Seidler,
architect

The new rules required that, in addition to fulfilling all of her college requirements, Patricia now needed two years' worth of professional experience in order to get licensed. However, because she had been very careful in what school she attended and in making sure she got "real world" experience through internships, this wasn't a problem for Patricia. But that doesn't mean it wasn't hard work!

Cool Careers: Product Designers

People who have training or experience in architecture can choose to follow many different career paths. Instead of becoming an architect, some people might choose to become product designers.

In product design, you must create a product for a business to sell. To do this, you need to think about what people need and how to fulfill that need creatively and practically.

Does this sound familiar? It is just like what an architect does, but on a smaller scale. Product designers need to think of an idea, draft plans, understand how a product will work and fit together, and then sell the idea. It requires working both creatively and scientifically. Product designers need to be good at both art and math.

Ask & Answer

To become an architect, you have to pass many exams. Do you think it is important for all licensed architects to pass these exams? Why or why not?

Patricia had to take seven national-level exams, called the Architecture Registration Examination (ARE), to get licensed. Plus, to become an architect in California, she had to take an additional test called the California Supplemental Examination (CSE). Finally, after studying for and taking all of these exams, Patricia was a licensed architect! This process took several years to complete.

PROFESSIONAL ARCHITECT!

After passing all of these exams, Patricia began working at a small architectural firm. She enjoyed the experiences she had there, particularly because she felt comfortable asking questions about anything and everything. But this began to change when she had been there for a while.

As Patricia says, "My curiosity and hunger to learn the 'whys' of what we do were perceived as ignorance or as a challenge." Patricia wanted to learn everything she could about the field, but some of her colleagues didn't want to help her learn. This was frustrating for her.

Despite this challenge, Patricia learned a great deal while working there and at other small firms. She became particularly interested in firms where the plumbing and mechanical and structural engineering were done in-house. This means that different architects in one firm specialize in adding plumbing into buildings, or incorporating other mechanical designs, such as elevators, into the project.

Maya Lin

Maya Lin knew success from a young age. While still a 21-year-old student at Yale University, she won an important design competition, beating out 1,441 other architects!

Her design became the Vietnam Veterans Memorial, an important tribute to Americans who lost their lives while fighting in the Vietnam War between 1955 and its end in 1975.

The Vietnam Veterans Memorial
photo credit: Derek Key

Patricia worked on projects that ranged from modernizing public school buildings to designing U.S. post offices. Her work included commercial projects for developers and "big box" projects. Commercial and "big box" architects work on designing and building large stores, such as Walmart and Ikea, and even shopping malls.

Maya designed a long, V-shaped wall made of black stone, upon which the names of all of those who died during the war are engraved. This important

photo credit: Forgemind ArchiMedia

project was completed in 1982. Today, it is one of the most popular tourist destinations in Washington, DC, receiving thousands of visitors a year. Maya owns her own architectural firm, Maya Lin Studio, in New York City.

66 The process I go through in the art and the architecture, I actually want it to be almost childlike. Sometimes, I think it's magical. 99

—Maya Lin

Patricia liked the fact that she could work on a broad range of projects and learn from people with different areas of expertise. But there was a downside to working at these small architectural firms: project deadlines. When a deadline was coming up to finalize a project, everyone in a small firm would "feel the weight" of it. They would often have to work far more than 40 hours each week. And if any team member got sick and had to take a day off, the whole team would feel the stress.

She says, "At the small firms, I gained a wealth of knowledge. Generally speaking, small firms are known for not paying very well, but for offering a broad range of experiences. A downside of working at a small firm is that the weight of the project deadlines, whether large or small, would be felt by everyone in the office."

Patricia points out that she liked working closely with her colleagues in this way, despite the stress. "I've found that small firms tend to be more efficient than larger firms," she says. "There is better communication among the members of the team and, in my experience, I always got the sense that we were all in it together."

After several years at small firms, Patricia began working at larger firms. There, she focused more on health care architecture, medical office buildings, and clinics.

This means that she worked to design the buildings you might use when you are sick and need to visit the doctor or if you are injured and need to go to the hospital. Designing buildings for health care services requires special knowledge of what kinds of structures are needed in the medical field. Patricia enjoyed doing this work.

Cool Careers:
Construction Managers

Construction management is an interesting career path to follow for those interested in architecture. If you want to pursue this career, you better get your hard hat on! Construction managers oversee the planning, design, and construction of a project, much like project architects do. However, construction managers typically spend more time at construction sites actually building with materials.

Learn about five inspirational women in construction management here.

Lowe's 5 Women success 🔍

After six years of working in this field, she realized that it was time for a change. She wanted more opportunity to move up the career ladder. And, as always, Patricia was curious to learn more about different parts of architecture.

Today, Patricia works as a project architect at a small firm. She loves what she does because she gets to see projects through from start to finish. This means working "from early schematic designs all the way through construction and completion."

Patricia has a good relationship with the principal, or owner, of the firm. Her boss trusts her work, and she now holds a more senior position. But it also requires juggling, as Patricia must work on several projects at once. In addition, she also mentors those on her team and gives advice to younger and less-experienced architects.

Patricia says, "My favorite part of my job is being a part of intangible ideas becoming a reality. I love the transformation of plans drawn on paper becoming a physical space that can be touched, seen, and experienced."

Patricia particularly enjoys the "construction administration" phase of her work. This is when the project is finally being built and Patricia gets to visit the site regularly. She loves to watch her hard work reach completion.

But that doesn't mean that Patricia, and women in general, don't face challenges in the field. Patricia mentions that she finds that both men and women tend to be "less accepting" of younger women in the field. It is encouraging to see that this is changing with younger generations.

However, she has advice for young women who are interested in entering the field of architecture.

"Young women should know that there may always be disparity in the field of architecture, but this doesn't mean that we should bow out and let the men take care of business. Women in architecture offer a perspective and skillset that is different from that of men in architecture, and what we women bring to the table is extremely useful in the kind of work that architects do."

Sometimes, Patricia says, she is cut off when she is talking. Sometimes, her proposals are not taken seriously by male colleagues.

The Missing 32 Percent

Women make up only between 15 and 18 percent of all licensed architects in the United States. A project called The Missing 32 Percent, which is part of the Equity by Design organization, aims to change that statistic.

Started in 2011, Equity by Design is a "call to action to realize the goal of equitable practice for everyone, advance the profession, and communicate the value of architecture to society." The group's vision is to achieve an "equitable practice" of 50 percent women among all licensed architects in the United States. The organization holds conferences and other events, conducts studies, and offers a great deal of information for women who are interested in joining the field.

Hear architect Rosa Sheng speak about equity in architecture and about women in the field here.

equity architecture YouTube 🔍

66 Focus and be open to possibilities—
don't be put off by the aggression of others.
Think things through, quietly get things done,
and communicate clearly, always taking into
account the position of other parties. 99

—Kathryn Findley,
architect

She also notices that, occasionally, something she mentions is dismissed, but when a male colleague mentions the same thing, it is accepted by the team. It can be frustrating, Patricia notes. But the rewards are great—seeing one's ideas built into a final project that can better the lives of an entire community!

Patricia has lots of advice for girls who are interested in joining her field one day. There are many organizations for women and girls who are interested in careers in architecture. Patricia suggests it's a good idea to reach out to one in your area.

Through these organizations, you can make connections with other women who are in the field. It's important, Patricia states, to ask them for advice— and don't be afraid to ask lots of questions!

ACE Mentoring Program

The Architecture, Construction, and Engineering (ACE) mentoring program reaches more than 8,000 high school students annually and pairs them with experienced mentors in the fields of construction and design. In addition, the program provides financial support to each student in the program through scholarships and grants that they can use for their studies. So far, it has awarded more than $14 million in scholarships to its participants! For more information, and to find an ACE program near you, check out its website at www.acementor.org.

You might develop some nice friendships through doing this, as Patricia has done. In particular, an Architecture, Construction, and Engineering (ACE) mentoring program would be very helpful to young students interested in architecture.

Finally, Patricia states that she is an advocate for all those who have found passions outside of architecture, all while pursuing a career in the field. She didn't take art or drafting in high school and decided to focus instead on music, which enriched her life in a different way.

As Patricia says, "There will be time for learning to draft, art and color theory, architecture history, and spatial composition" once you are in your college architecture program.

Cultivate your passion for architecture, Patricia concludes, but make sure to also focus on all the other fun things you enjoy doing. Music, art, and sports can also enrich your life and, perhaps, even make you into a better architect one day.

66 I used to not like being called a 'woman architect.' I'm an architect, not just a woman architect. The guys used to tap me on the head and say, 'You're okay for a girl.' But I see an incredible amount of need from other women for reassurance that it can be done, so I don't mind anymore. **99**

—Zaha Hadid,
architect

CHAPTER 3

Farida Abu-Bakare

Becoming a licensed architect takes a very, very long time. In addition to many years of school, architects need to work for several years in the field before taking licensing exams. Farida Abu-Bakare is an intern architect, which means that she has completed her hours of internship experience and has begun writing her licensing exams. She already has a great deal of experience, and once she passes her exams, she will be even more unstoppable!

The Doha, Qatar, skyline in the morning

photo credit: Francisco Anzola

Farida was born on April 19, 1988, in Doha, Qatar. The country of Qatar is located on the northeast side of a landmass called the Arabian Peninsula in Asia. It is surrounded by Saudi Arabia to the south and west and by the waters of the Persian Gulf to the north and east.

Farida's parents are both of Nigerian descent, although her mother was born in England, while her father was born in Nigeria. Farida's father went to school in Canada and obtained his citizenship there when he was still a young man, so Farida was born with Canadian citizenship as well.

Farida has three sisters, Ayesha, Tahira, and Amal. Her father is a physician and an endocrinologist who specializes in internal medicine. Farida's mother worked as an accountant. Then she earned a degree in human resources and a graduate degree in business administration and now works as a consultant.

Farida remembers that her mother always had an "artistic streak." She loved to make pencil drawings and continues to create watercolor paintings today. Both Farida's mother and father have always encouraged her to follow her passion for art. Do you think art and business have any similarities? Why might Farida's mother have been interested in both?

From a young age, Farida felt that her desire to pursue architecture as a career was a perfect blending of "the practicality of math" and "the impractical and creative nature of art and design."

Ask & Answer

Where are you and your family from? How does your heritage inform who you are and who you would like to become?

As a young girl, Farida was interested in several video games, particularly *SimCity*, in which you can construct towns and cities, and *SIMs*, where you can create homes for people and control their daily lives. She loved designing spaces and creating homes and towns in these virtual worlds.

Farida also loved technology and art. She enjoyed painting and sketching by hand, as well as computer design. Farida's mother noticed both her artistic streak and her strength in math. She provided Farida with extra tutoring in mathematics, which allowed Farida to further excel.

Farida remembers a gift that changed her life when she was just 10 years old. She received a series of block stamps that could be used to create a tower. It was called *Fun with Architecture*.

Farida didn't know yet what architecture was. When her mother explained to her that architects must excel in both math and art, Farida resolved that she would pursue both of her passions through a career in architecture.

Unfortunately, Farida was not as encouraged by her teachers as she was by her parents. Many of Farida's teachers simply thought that a girl could not grow up to be an architect.

66 Women are the real architects of society. 99

—Harriet Beecher Stowe,
author and abolitionist

Farida reflects, "I do not believe that there were any women in the [field of] architecture at the time, let alone of my racial background, besides Zaha Hadid, who was only well known within the architecture and design community. I believe that my teachers didn't think it was possible for me because they had never seen it before."

FINDING HER PLACE

Zaha Hadid became a role model for Farida. Zaha was born in 1950 in Iraq, a country near Farida's home country of Qatar, and became one of the most important and influential architects in the world. Few women had achieved such fame in architecture before Zaha. You can learn more about Zaha on pages 58 and 59.

In 2004, just before Farida began her undergraduate studies, she came across an article in *Vogue* magazine about the famous architect. Zaha had recently been awarded the highest prize in architecture, called the Pritzker Prize.

The Heydar Aliyev Cultural Center in Baku, Azerbaijan, designed by Zaha Hadid

"Reading about her approach to life, architecture, and seeing all that she had accomplished was a huge moment of self-realization for me," Farida says. "I knew right then and there that anything was possible."

The next year, Farida left home to begin her bachelor of architectural studies at Carleton University in Ottawa, Canada. The program was very challenging and most of the students there were older than Farida. They had already gone through architectural technology college before this program.

People who work in architectural technology use computer-based programs and other technology designed to help architects. They often draft designs and prepare estimates of the costs of building materials. They serve as an important link between architects and construction crews.

Although she struggled at first, Farida had always excelled in school and this time was no different. She received her bachelor's degree in the summer of 2009. One of the most inspiring encounters of Farida's college career came when she met with an architect and family friend named Mohammed Lawal. Mohammed is a practicing architect in the United States. Farida visited him there so she could see what he did and ask him for advice.

Mohammed explained that, from the beginning, Farida would face many challenges in the profession as a woman—particularly a woman with African heritage. He gave her a copy of the March 2007 issue of *Architect* magazine and said it was important for her to know the challenges she might face.

The magazine's cover story focused on the lack of licensed African-American female architects. "The shocking demographic of 0.2 percent motivated me more than anything else to keep going," Farida says. Farida knew what she wanted, and would not stop until she had achieved her goal.

Ask & Answer

Have you ever felt very discouraged? How did you overcome this feeling?

After completing her bachelor's degree at the age of 21, Farida immediately pursued her masters degree in architecture at Ryerson University in Toronto, Canada, in the fall of 2009. While completing her master's degree, she embarked on several internships at local firms. Farida completed her master's degree in 2012.

Zaha Hadid

Zaha Hadid was born on October 31, 1950, in Baghdad, Iraq. She studied math at the American University of Beirut, Lebanon, before moving to London in 1972. In London, she studied at the famous Architectural Association School of Architecture. Her teachers have described her as one of the most promising students they had ever taught. One teacher stated, "She couldn't care [less] about tiny details. Her mind was on the broader pictures . . . and she was right."

66 My work is not within the accepted box. Maybe because I am a woman. Also an Arab. There was a certain prejudice about these things. 99

—Zaha Hadid,
architect

In Canada, to be a licensed architect, you need not only a bachelor's degree, but also a master's degree from an accredited school. After this, a young architect can become an "intern architect." This begins the process of completing licensure, which is the process to become a professional and certified architect.

After graduation, Zaha opened up her own architectural firm in 1980 in London. Quickly, she earned a reputation as being an innovative and daring architect

photo credit: Simone Cecchetti

with designs based on curves and continuity instead of straight lines. Her buildings, including the Broad Art Museum in Michigan and the London Olympics Aquatics Center, can be found all around the world.

Zaha was the first female architect to ever receive the Pritzker Architecture Prize, in 2004. She passed away at the age of 65 in 2016.

Check out some of Zaha Hadid's most famous designs and buildings here.

Arcspace Zaha Hadid 🔎

You need to complete a certain number of hours before you can even take the needed licensing exams, which takes about two to three years of full-time work. Then, a young architect in Canada must pass a series of four exams, which cover the entire architectural and design process. Only after this can you apply for a license and become a licensed architect.

Farida experienced many challenges during this drawn-out process. First of all, she was the youngest in her graduate program. This was largely because, due to a weak economy and a lack of jobs, many of her classmates had many years of architectural experience but were unable to find work. This meant that people with years of experience working in architecture-related fields were going back to college for a graduate degree.

Farida always felt that she was lagging behind these students because they were older and, in some ways, more advanced than her. However, she pushed through these challenges and would not let anything stop her.

Farida credits her ability to follow through on her dreams to her parents. They were her "biggest cheerleaders" throughout the entire process. Her parents always provided her with plenty of encouragement, even during the most difficult, darkest moments.

STEPPING STONES

Upon graduating, Farida had a list of three firms that she liked—and she was determined to work for one of them. She applied for every job posting she saw at these firms for several months during the final semester of her graduate studies.

However, it became apparent that she could not compete with others who had more years of professional experience than her. She was not selected for any of the positions she applied for.

Then, in the summer of 2012, Farida was finally hired for a job she longed for—as an office administrator and designer at HOK in Toronto, Canada. HOK is a global design, architecture, engineering, and planning firm. It has 23 offices around the world, including in Toronto, New York, London, and Hong Kong.

Ask & Answer

Have you ever not been chosen for something that you really wanted? How did you feel? Did you keep trying to achieve your goal even after your first rejection? What about your second and third rejections?

Farida accepted the position knowing that it would be a stepping stone. She knew that she would not be doing everything she wanted to accomplish right away. But she could use her experience at this firm to delve deeper into her passion.

During her first three months at HOK, Farida did all she could to display her architectural skills. She hoped that this would lead to being able to take on more responsibilities. It worked!

Farida was promoted to a position in the studio where she was able to design with the urban planning and architecture teams at the firm.

Farida wasn't content to stay at this level, though. She wanted to continue pushing forward and excelling in her career. Less than six months later, she received a coveted position as an intern architect at HOK in Calgary, Canada. Finally, she would be able to log her hours toward her architectural license.

Farida continues to work as an intern architect, now in the HOK office in Atlanta, Georgia. She has honed her skills and has gained specialization in science and technology.

Her clients are primarily pharmaceutical companies and higher education institutions, such as universities and technical colleges. Pharmaceutical companies make medicine and other drugs, and they need architects who can help plan and design specialized laboratories for them.

Farida spends most of her day at the computer in her office, where she uses a variety of Autodesk software. This software allows architects to design, draft, and model different projects in both two dimensions (2-D) and three dimensions (3-D). It helps her to design laboratories and other science-centered buildings.

What Tools Do Architects Use?

Architects use a variety of tools to program, design, draft, and construct their structures. Some of these tools are at the cutting edge of technology, while others have been around for hundreds of years. Many architects use software made by Autodesk to draft and model using computer simulations in both 2-D and 3-D. However, many architects still draft by hand, depending on the project and the phase of the design process. In addition to relying on computers and software to construct their designs, architects use pencils, tracing paper, compasses, triangles, slide rulers, and calculators. Today's tools of an architect's trade are a true blend of old and new.

> 66 Architecture is a visual art, and the buildings speak for themselves. 99
>
> **—Julia Morgan,**
> the first female architect to be licensed in California

In addition to working at her computer, Farida spends a lot of time on conference calls, answering emails, and in meetings. These meetings are usually spent discussing project guidelines and deadlines in collaboration with engineers and contractors.

Farida also makes weekly and monthly site visits, both locally and regionally. Some projects can require a lot of travel, depending on the design phase! This is when she gets to step away from her computer and break out the hard hat, safety glasses, vest, and boots to coordinate and collaborate with the engineers and contractors.

Being on site is especially rewarding for Farida, as she gets to see the progress of her work firsthand and watch her design come to life.

Farida sees each project from the initial programming and schematic design through to design development and construction documents. This means that she designs and models buildings and then must come up with plans that show construction crews how to build them. Every day, Farida is focused on meeting deadlines and milestones—she sometimes gets very busy!

MAKING A DIFFERENCE

Farida still has many goals that she wants to pursue. Giving back to help others is important to her. She would love to work as a consultant within an organization such as the United Nations (UN).

The UN is a large organization made up of many different countries that all work together toward worldwide peace. The UN runs an agency called the United Nations Human Settlements Program, which consults with architects, designers, and urban planners to evaluate and address disaster risks in cities. The program promotes and develops sustainable human settlement and urban development.

This means that architects can help build cities and towns for people who live in areas that might experience higher risks of natural disasters. These disasters include earthquakes and tsunamis. There are man-made disasters as well, such as war. The program's architects, designers, and urban planners work hard to make sure that everyone around the world has adequate shelter. The mission is for people to be safe and secure in their communities.

There is no doubt that Farida will continue to make a difference, both in her career and in the world at large. But that doesn't mean that she hasn't faced— or that she doesn't continue to face—obstacles, particularly as a woman in the field.

> **66** I have practiced [architecture] now for 40 years, and the percentage of women in leadership roles in the profession has improved only a small percentage in that time. **99**
>
> **—Rebecca Barnes,**
> architect

Farida mentions that being a female architect can be challenging, as "you must always be very conscious of how you present yourself to both coworkers and clients." Farida continues, "It can sometimes be exhausting to have to constantly prove your worth, knowledge, and very existence to everyone all the time."

Oftentimes, Farida explains, women in the field are not taken as seriously as men. This is particularly true in the case of younger women, such as Farida, who are expected to work twice as hard as anyone else to prove themselves in the field. Farida suggests that one way young women can deal with this pressure is by seeking out a mentor. A mentor is someone who has experience in a particular field and helps to teach and guide younger, less-experienced people.

"Mentorship from an early age is so important, as the guidance and motivation a mentor provides is unparalleled," Farida states. "Women are a minority in this male-dominated field, so, unfortunately, constantly proving yourself is the reality. Having a mentor is a huge confidence booster and, paired with good guidance, you are unstoppable!"

Farida recognizes the particular challenges she faces as a minority woman in her field. She says, "We need to also realize that representation matters—women need to seek out each other and seek out and recruit young women to our profession."

African-American women are much less represented than Caucasian women in the field. It can be very discouraging for young African-American women who do not find anyone who looks like them—or has in-depth knowledge of the particular challenges they face—in their career.

"We must be the diversity we seek," Farida advises. "For the field to become less challenging for women, we need to band together, speak out about the issues we face, and support and empower one another to engage in those uncomfortable conversations that lead to change."

Farida says that, personally, she has overcome many of the challenges she has faced by "never taking no for an answer." She is headstrong and determined and meets every challenge with conviction.

Ask & Answer

Do you have someone you consider to be a mentor to you? How have they helped you? What are you grateful to them for?

African-American Women in Architecture

According to *Architect* magazine, the number of African-American female architects has quadrupled in recent years. That's amazing! However, African-American women are still not well represented in the field. Only 196 African-American women are licensed architects in the United States. That means they make up only 0.2 percent of all architects in the country.

What can be done about this? Architectural schools are trying to recruit a diverse population of students and professors. It is important that younger generations of African-American women who are interested in the field see themselves among the ranks of the architects they admire. Theodore Landsmark, who chaired the American Institute of Architects' diversity committee, says that the field is slowly diversifying with these new efforts. "It is safe to say that within the next decade, most of the clients will not look like what most of the architects look like today," he says. That's a good thing.

You can learn more about the AIA's work for diversity and inclusion here.

AIA equity diversity 🔍

Farida admits, "My intuition, determination, and tenacity [have] brought me where I am today. I never give up and always trust my instincts. I feel these strengths came from having such a strong support system and having the confidence and motivation to keep going [even when things got tough].

"My advice to young girls and young women is not to be afraid to be uncomfortable and do not be afraid to fail," Farida continues. "We must stop being so afraid of being uncomfortable, as discomfort breeds so much growth and strength. You should instead lean into discomfort and learn from it. We must stop teaching that failure is a negative outcome. Always challenge yourself—without failing at something, you will never know what you excel in."

Farida cites Oprah Winfrey, the talk show host, actress, and businesswoman, as an inspiration. She repeats Oprah's quote, "There is no such thing as failure. Failure is just life trying to move us in another direction," as being particularly inspirational.

Oprah Winfrey
photo credit: Alan Light

"Trust your intuition," Farida states. "Pay attention to your passions, and once you discover what you are most passionate about, pursue a career in it. Young girls and young women should be aware that architecture is a path that you can consider no matter what your background is."

Farida knows many colleagues who came to architecture from different passions and experiences. There are those who excelled in mathematics before pursuing classes in art. Other colleagues studied music and art history before falling in love with architecture later in life. "That's the beauty of architecture," Farida says. "[The] path toward becoming an architect has no rules, and you can explore and discover yourself for as long as you like."

The sky's the limit for Farida, a young woman who is charting a new path through the field of architecture with determination and strength.

> 66 Architecture can't force people to connect, it can only plan the crossing points, remove barriers, and make the meeting places useful and attractive. 99
>
> **—Denise Scott Brown,**
> architect

CHAPTER 4
Maia Small

Throughout Maia Small's career in architecture, she has done it all. She has been an architect at both small and large firms, opened up her own architectural firm, and even taught architecture to college students. But Maia has found her calling as an urban designer in the city of San Francisco. This is yet another interesting career that architects can pursue—planning out cities to make sure the people who live there are happy and comfortable.

Maia Small was born on January 30, 1973, in Portland, Oregon, to Carol and Enoch Small. Maia was an only child. She grew up in the quiet landscape of a town called Kings Valley, with equal amounts of woods and farms. As of 2010, there were only 65 residents of Kings Valley!

The house she grew up in was designed and built by her parents, though they weren't architects. Later on, Maia would gain half- and step-siblings after her parents divorced and remarried.

The house her parents built in Kings Valley, as well as the second house Maia grew up in, would influence the rest of Maia's life. Maia says, "They were both made up of mostly natural materials—mostly wood—and full of warmth and texture. They were both small compared to what you might see now, but they were complex—with lots of small levels, lofts, ladders, decks, and many spaces where the ceilings were high and open. These houses felt like they held secrets and always beckoned for discovery."

Ask & Answer

Where did you grow up? How do you think where you grew up influenced the person you would become?

> 66 At about five, I knew I was going to be an architect because my mother had studied architecture. I thought it was women's work. I had a proprietary feeling about architecture. I could own it because my mother owned it. 99

—Denise Scott Brown,
architect

Maia was able to watch her parents as they built, fixed, and maintained these houses. But Maia was preoccupied with another part of living in these special structures: exploration.

"The intricate structures offered places that were only available to me: closets, corners, under furniture, or in crawl spaces or on top of wood piles, sheds, or even roofs," Maia says. "My parents encouraged my exploration and, as an only child, I spent hours making forts with pillows, blankets, sheets, and furniture, along with roaming outside in the woods with friends."

It was this unique space that her parents built with their own hands that led Maia to discover and build with materials, too. Her father cut and sanded extra planks of wood that he gave to Maia. For years, Maia would take these planks and build her own structures in the back yard of her house. She still has them today, and her young daughter enjoys playing and building with them, too, when she heads to her grandparents' house.

EARLIEST MEMORIES

Maia's childhood is filled with rich memories that involve watching and discovering the joys of building. Her earliest memories were of visiting the site where her mother and father were building their second house, in Corvallis, Oregon.

"My dad brought me through the woods and we came upon a low grid of concrete walls. He walked me around and explained how this area would be my room, this one my bathroom, and this other one was for my parents. He was pointing just to dirt! How could that possibly be my room? Yet I watched the house go up—the concrete walls would begin to hold wood framing for floors, and more vertical framing for walls, then ceiling beams would come on top, and eventually, the whole project was skinned until you needed a door to get in! It was a magical process—from land and pieces came a HOME."

While other children Maia's age played with dolls, Maia made furniture and created backyard structures with wooden planks. Maia credits her parents with encouraging her passion in different ways.

Her father was a biophysicist. This is someone who studies the body using the properties of physics. He shared his scientific mind and curiosity with his daughter. He loved making things and figuring out practical solutions to problems.

Maia's mother is a writer and editor who imparted the importance of clear communication and intuition to her daughter. This is important for architects because they don't work with materials alone. Architects must present their work to their clients and colleagues and express the importance of their designs. Maia's mother also encouraged her in artistic pursuits, including drawing and painting.

Maia clearly remembers the moment she decided she wanted to be an architect. At around the age of six, Maia had wanted to be a paleontologist or entomologist. A paleontologist is a scientist who studies fossils, while an entomologist is a scientist who studies bugs.

But that year, she built her own desk to use for her art projects. She loved this project, and soon she had changed her mind—she would become an architect!

Maia was naturally good in both the subjects of math and art. As Maia grew up, her parents continued to foster her passion.

Ask & Answer

What was the first career you wanted to pursue when you grew up? How has this evolved over time?

Maia began to participate more and more in her father's construction projects, including settling concrete in formwork, sanding woodwork, and working with power tools. There wasn't anything in the construction process that she eventually was not familiar with.

Denise Scott Brown

Denise Scott Brown (1931–) is one of the most famous—and most influential—architects of the twentieth century. Born in Northern Rhodesia (a region that today is called Zambia, a country in central Africa) in 1931, Denise knew she wanted to be an architect from the age of five. Denise studied at the University of the Witwatersrand in South Africa before moving to London to work with the architect Frederick Gibberd. She was accepted into the Architectural Association School of Architecture (known as the AA) in London for a graduate degree in architecture. The AA is the oldest architectural school in England and one of the most prestigious in the world. While there, she experimented with combining her love for architecture with her passion for women's rights. She wanted to use architectural design to create a more equal society for all people.

In 1958, Denise moved to Pennsylvania to study and then work at the University of Pennsylvania.

There were other formative moments in Maia's path to becoming an architect. One was a trip to New York City to visit her grandparents when she was five. Maia marveled at the skyscrapers, the environment, and the tightly packed city streets filled with many different kinds of people.

photo credit: Columbia GSAPP

Eventually, she and her husband, Robert Venturi, created the firm Scott Brown and Venturi. Together, Denise and Robert innovated ways of designing cities by taking into account population size and movement, as well as other social and economic factors.

In 1991, Robert Venturi won the Pritzker Architecture Prize—although his partner and wife was not named as a recipient of the prize with him. Denise didn't attend the ceremony in protest. She has continued to speak out against discrimination against female architects since then.

You can read more about the Pritzker committee's controversial decision here.

Pritzker Prize Brown 🔎

Cool Careers: Construction

Working in construction is similar in some ways to working in architecture. While architects work hard to plan, draw, and model designs for buildings and other structures, construction workers actually bring these designs and models to life.

Construction workers work at construction sites, where they use a range of tools to build. They also must clean and prepare a site before building, load and unload material, and follow detailed construction plans. Construction workers need to use their physical strength as well as their brains to be successful!

While many people traditionally think of construction work as a career for men, more and more women are joining the ranks. Construction work is typically flexible, reliable, satisfying, and well paid. And many women, like Maia, enjoy working with their hands and then seeing the satisfaction of their hard work in a finished building!

Maia especially remembers visiting the World Trade Center. "Standing at the base of nearly the tallest building in the world in 1978 was overwhelming, and I walked right up to the face of the building and looked up as if I was looking at an infinite plane," Maia remembers. "It was sublime—both glorious and scary. How could people have even thought of such an amazing thing and then actually built it?"

Another trip that solidified Maia's interest in architecture was when she visited Spain with her family at the age of 11. Spending three weeks with her mother and stepfamily driving across the Spanish countryside, Maia was able to take in the small churches, monuments, houses, and larger cities.

In Barcelona, Maia was amazed by the cathedral there, while in Grenada she loved seeing the grottos and fountains she saw at Alhambra. "I imagined the families that had lived here and the people who had designed it," she said.

Ask & Answer

What is the most exciting trip you have ever been on? What do you remember most about it and how has it changed your life?

Alhambra in Grenada, Spain

From then on, Maia would marvel over large cities and the people who designed and lived in them. "I wanted to understand how such urban organisms actually came to be," Maia explains.

A BUDDING ARCHITECT

Maia's passion developed further in school, where she excelled at math from an early age. Maia also became interested in computers and coding when she was a young teenager. Coding was another language that she could use to construct things that were in her mind. Ever since then, Maia says, computers have played an important role in her professional life. She uses them for drawing, modeling, and writing.

> **66** Cities have the capability of providing something for everybody, only because, and only when, they are created by everybody. **99**

> **—Jane Jacobs,**
> author and activist

Maia also had many hobbies. She was the captain of the volleyball team, second cellist in the youth orchestra, ran the ski club, and was head of an academic club. In volleyball and orchestra, in particular, Maia learned how to balance her determination and her thirst for excellence with the necessary give-and-take of teamwork.

"As an only child who did not grow up around many other kids," Maia states, "I learned a lot about teamwork—about finding shared values, understanding and relating to how other people see themselves, that sometimes yielding the floor or honoring others was a form of leadership or collaboration."

Maia ended her career in high school with a near-perfect grade point average and credit for having taken college courses. She also had leadership experience and the ambition to get into the top architectural schools in the country.

However, she met with several obstacles before applying to college. One obstacle came from her guidance counselor, who told her that she should focus on community college and take extra drafting courses. "This is not . . . the advice that she gave my male classmate, who had exactly the same credentials," says Maia.

Despite this bad advice, Maia easily achieved her goal. She was one of 10 students in the state to be accepted into the architectural program at the University of California Berkeley. While at Berkeley, Maia took a range of classes, not only in architecture and math, but also in science, art history, language, and writing.

Maia was surprised that architects are expected to learn so many subjects! However, she enjoyed the subjects themselves, as well as the passion her professors imparted when they taught them.

Each of these classes influenced how Maia would think about architecture. "Learning to write helped me understand the importance of having an argument or point of view; art history helped me understand how people developed creativity and craft to express their culture, time, and place; environmental science helped me to understand resources, natural systems, and how what we do impacts them," Maia says.

UC Berkeley campus in Berkeley, California
photo credit: Charlie Nguyen

College was just the start of learning to think critically and employ all of her experiences in service of her passion. After graduating from Berkeley with a bachelor's degree in architecture with highest honors, Maia was anxious to begin working in the field. She had previously interned for architects and wanted to gain more professional experience.

66 Architecture is like a mythical fantastic. It has to be experienced. It can't be described. We can draw it up and we can make models of it, but it can only be experienced as a complete whole. 99

—Maya Lin,
architect of the Vietnam Veterans Memorial

Maia was fortunate to land a position working for the architect Mark Cavagnero, a young architect who had his own small firm, where he worked on large public buildings. Working among a small team of five architects, Maia was required to know about each deadline and be involved in nearly all client communications. She saw all drawings and designs that went into and out of the small office.

During her time at this firm, Maia was able to work on large projects, such as master planning the de Young Museum at the Fine Arts Museums of San Francisco. She also worked on smaller projects, including designing elevator interiors for the California Palace of the Legion of Honor.

In addition to learning about architecture itself, Maia gained invaluable experience learning how to work on a team. She also learned about the business side of architecture, including how to manage clients, billing, and insurance. Mark continues to be an important mentor in Maia's life today.

Ask & Answer

What do you think are the benefits of working for small companies? For larger companies?

> 66 We try to find what we cannot imagine perfectly. If I can see the final results immediately, I lose interest. 99
>
> **—Kazuyo Sejima,**
> architect

After two years, Maia traveled to New York City once again to begin her graduate career at Columbia University. She chose Columbia University because of the innovative work architects at Columbia were doing using new architectural software.

She also enjoyed being a part of the thriving city of New York while learning about cities. How such large cities are planned and developed and how their growth can be managed through architectural solutions were topics that fascinated Maia. Earning this graduate degree gave her more technical knowledge about the field.

After receiving her master's degree from Columbia and an additional year of work, Maia had enough experience to take her licensing exams. She had to take nine exams in all, and finished taking them about six years after her graduate degree.

Maia explains, "Like doctors, no one can say they are an architect unless they have a license—while you may hear of the term 'licensed architect,' it is redundant!"

"Being an architect means that you are responsible for the life and safety of the people in the buildings you design. So, to be qualified, you must have earned accredited college degrees, gained experience in an office while overseen by an architect, have qualified to take the licensing exams, and taken them successfully."

Since Maia has passed these exams, she has to renew her license every two years, which includes showing additional educational credits to ensure that she is current in her field.

Maia began her post-graduate career working for a famous architect who required that his staff work long hours and weekends. It was very stressful for Maia— but not because she wasn't used to working hard. The problem was that what was expected was not always effectively communicated to the staff.

When Maia was just 26, she was able to lead her first project, designing the first urban national park in Canada. This was not only a very important project, it was also part of a competition between five large architectural firms around the world.

While her team didn't win the competition, they completed the project successfully. Maia was impressed with what she and her team had been able to accomplish together.

Cool Careers: Professor of Architecture

Professors of architecture teach university students what they know about the field. They must be comfortable speaking in public and must enjoy working with students. Usually, professors of architecture have worked for several years as professional architects. They must also have a graduate degree in the field.

Teaching architecture to younger generations can be inspiring and fulfilling. Professors of architecture can also pursue their own projects on the side, although they might not have the resources to take on large-scale projects. However, professors have the satisfaction of knowing that they are shaping new generations of architects who will design and build wonderful things!

Read more here about how to become a professor of architecture.

succeed as young professor of architecture 🔎

After spending a year at this firm, Maia decided upon a change of pace. She moved to Knoxville in order to teach architecture at the University of Tennessee. She was excited to do academic work and design projects on her own. But, after several years there, she realized that she craved the opportunity to apply more of what she had learned in school.

Next, Maia moved from Tennessee to Rhode Island, where she established her own architectural practice with her husband.

She ran her own practice for about 10 years. Maia worked on all kinds of projects, from downtown revitalization and streetscape improvements to designing bike lanes. She even worked on larger projects, such as building parks and bridges.

Maia often volunteered her time and worked with politicians and state agencies on local planning that would help make communities better. These projects were all very rewarding for Maia, who enjoyed making the lives of those in the community better. However, she still faced difficulties, particularly as a female small business owner.

"The biggest obstacle I faced was low expectations," Maia says. "People often assumed, because I was a younger woman, that I was in a meeting as an assistant, not as the leader.

Ask & Answer

Have you ever felt like others held low expectations for you? How did this make you feel?

"I found that once I commanded the room through knowledge, confidence, and ease, that awkwardness quickly would drop away. Then, people were very comfortable with my leadership or participation."

URBAN DESIGNER

In 2013, Maia left her practice in Rhode Island and moved to the Bay Area of California to take a job with the City of San Francisco's Planning Department as a staff architect. Maia works as one of the lead urban designers and a newly appointed team leader for a growing group of architects.

Together, Maia and her team develop urban design policies. The purpose is to help the city grow at an appropriate and sustainable pace.

So far, Maia has worked on more than 600 projects during the course of three years in the Planning Department. These projects range from small houses to 900-foot-tall towers and everything in between.

San Francisco, California

In order to complete these projects, "We think about how all of the parts of a city go together. We think about how that creates and protects neighborhoods and the people who live in them."

Maia's day-to-day life as an urban designer involves a range of different duties. Sometimes, she works by herself, but she also meets with people, both colleagues and clients. Maia draws at her desk and spends time looking over plans and seeing what might be missing in a project—such as open space or sidewalks. Part of her job involves writing detailed notes to one of many other planners.

Maia is proud that she has met the goals she set out for herself, not just to become a successful architect, but also to become a wife and a mother. This, however, has been one of the most challenging aspects of her professional life.

"Architecture is not a family-friendly business, which is why many women open their own offices—they have more choice in the type and pace of the work they do," Maia reflects. "Firms often promote working long hours and focusing only on work conversation. I found that after I had my daughter, it was nearly impossible to do everything necessary to run my practice anymore. I didn't want to just stick her with a nanny all day—I had her to raise and enjoy!"

At her current position, Maia says that she has flexible hours and a family-friendly environment where she can also focus on her passion for her work. She has found the perfect balance—a career that she enjoys and a family life that she has time for.

Ask & Answer

How do you imagine your life—and your career—will be 10 years from now? Twenty? Thirty?

Maia's Advice for Women

1. Exhibit more confidence in your skills. "Almost every time I bluffed my way into something, I could totally handle it," Maia says. She did not allow any insecurity to stop her.

2. Ask for raises and negotiate higher pay. In the past, Maia was offered a lower starting salary than male colleagues, but she was able to negotiate to a more equal pay rate.

3. If someone asks you to make coffee, make the worst coffee ever! "No one will ever ask you again," Maia says.

Maia believes that the system for women in architecture must be changed to allow women who would like families to have more flexibility. But she advises that change can also start with individual actions that women can take.

"I think the best you can do in the day-to-day is to be both very good at your job and at ease with your situation. Realize how much power you have by being smart and acting or speaking only when you really have something to contribute," Maia says.

"Be authentic to yourself, but learn how to listen and adapt. Be resilient when something isn't going well, and know how to calm yourself."

Maia advises those interested in pursuing architecture as a career to learn how to draw by hand while also learning computer coding. She suggests traveling and exploring differently built landscapes and cities. Furthermore, Maia states, "In a practical sense, you really need to learn almost everything to be an architect: math, science, language, art, social sciences, and physics."

Maia concludes, "I probably will never have my name on a building cornerstone, but my work feels invisibly and durably important." And, in the end, that matters more than anything else.

> 66 When we design buildings or cities,
> we have to understand the people and
> place, we have to have an idea about what
> we want to make, and we have to think about
> the effects, not only on that place, but on
> every consequence of our choices. 99
>
> **—Maia Small**

Timeline

Eighth Millennium BCE

- The earliest settlements, including Jericho in the modern-day Palestinian Territories, are built.

2600 BCE

- The Great Pyramid of Giza, an ancient architectural marvel, is built in Egypt.

700 BCE

- According to legend, the city of Rome is founded.

Around 30 BCE

- The Roman architect Vitruvius writes the first architectural treatise, entitled *De Architectura*.

Around 100 CE

- The Pantheon in Rome is completed.

1480s

- Both Vitruvius' *De Architectura* and Leon Battista Alberti's *De Re Aedificatoria* are published for the first time.

1660s

- King Louis XIV of France begins to build the Palace of Versailles, making it one of the largest and most impressive structures ever built.

1735

- Buckingham Palace is built.

1800

- The White House, in Washington, DC, is completed by planner Pierre L'Enfant and architect James Hoban.

1806

- The Arc de Triomphe is commissioned by Napoleon in Paris.

1873

- Mary L. Page (1849–1921) becomes the first woman to earn a degree in architecture in the United States when she graduates from the University of Illinois at Urbana-Champaign.

1888

- Louise Blanchard Bethune (1856–1913) becomes the first female architect to work professionally in the United States.

1891

- Sophia Hayden Bennett (1868–1953), at the age of 21, wins the design competition for the Women's Building at the Columbian Exhibition of the 1893 World's Fair.

1931

- The Empire State Building becomes the tallest building in the world.

1937

- Architect Frank Lloyd Wright (1867–1959) completes his iconic Fallingwater house in Bear Run, Pennsylvania.

1959

- Frank Lloyd Wright completes the Guggenheim Museum in New York City.

1973

- The towers of the World Trade Center open to the public in New York City.

1981

- At the age of 21, Maya Lin (1959–) wins the competition to design the Vietnam Veterans Memorial.

1985

- Norma Merrick Sklarek (1926–2012) is the first African American woman to build her own architecture firm and she is also the first African American woman to be licensed in architecture.

1991

- Robert Venturi (1925–) wins the Pritzker Prize, the top award in architecture. His partner and wife, Denise Scott Brown (1931–), boycotts the awards ceremony for not having been jointly awarded the prize.

2004

- Zaha Hadid (1950–2016) becomes the first woman and the first Iraqi to win the coveted Pritzker Prize.

2010

- The Burj Khalifa in Dubai, the United Arab Emirates, becomes the largest man-made structure in the world.

2013

- The Freedom Tower (still officially known as the World Trade Center) is completed, and is the tallest building in New York.

2016

- Zaha Hadid wins the prestigious Royal Institute of British Architects Royal Gold Medal. A few weeks later she passes away, on March 31.

Ask & Answer

Chapter 1

- Why do you think the ancient Egyptians decided to construct pyramids, instead of another shape?

- Today, some people around the world are designing tiny homes where people can live cheaply, sustainably, and simply. Would you ever live in a tiny home? Why or why not?

- Look around your home. Do you know who designed it and when? What are some things you like about the design of your home? What are some things you don't like?

- Think about your favorite building. It could be one you use every day or one you've only see on television. Why is it your favorite? What do you like about it?

Chapter 2

- Have you been in difficult situations with friends or family members? Do you feel as though these difficult times have made you stronger? Why?

- Do your parents pressure you to excel at school or in your hobbies? Even if it is sometimes frustrating, do you think their interest pushes you to do better?

- Do you share a particular hobby with a group of people? Has practicing your hobby with others made it more or less enjoyable for you?

- To become an architect, you have to pass many exams. Do you think it is important for all licensed architects to pass these exams? Why or why not?

- Patricia thinks that it is gradually becoming easier for women in traditionally male-dominated fields such as architecture. Why do you think this might be?

- What hobbies do you have that enrich your life, even if you don't think you'll pursue them as a career?

Chapter 3

- Where are you and your family from? How does your heritage inform who you are and who you would like to become?

- Are there any video games or other activities that you enjoy? Do you think you could take the skills you use in these games and use them in your career one day?

- Have you ever felt very discouraged? How did you overcome this feeling?

- Have you ever not been chosen for something that you really wanted? How did you feel? Did you keep trying to achieve your goal even after your first rejection? What about your second and third rejections?

- Do you have someone you consider to be a mentor to you? How have they helped you? What are you grateful to them for?

Chapter 4

- Where did you grow up? How do you think where you grew up influenced the person you would become?

- What was the first career you wanted to pursue when you grew up? How has this evolved over time?

- What is the most exciting trip you have ever been on? What do you remember most about it and how has it changed your life?

- What do you think are the benefits of working for small companies? For larger companies?

- Have you ever felt like others held low expectations for you? How did this make you feel?

- How do you imagine your life—and your career—will be 10 years from now? Twenty? Thirty?

abusive: offensive, insulting, or cruel.

accreditation: the process of showing that a person or organization is qualified to offer a particular service.

adequate: satisfactory or acceptable.

advisor: someone who gives advice.

advocate: to speak out for.

aggression: violent or overly bold behavior to another person.

archaeologist: a scientist who studies ancient people and their cultures by looking at what they left behind.

archaeology: the study of ancient people through the objects they left behind.

architect: an artist who designs buildings.

architecture: the style or look of a building.

Art Nouveau: a style of architecture, which focused on linear designs and natural forms, that became popular in the United States and Europe in the late nineteenth and early twentieth century.

artifact: an object made by humans for a purpose.

Baroque: the design and architecture of the seventeenth and eighteen century in Europe, characterized by many ornate details.

BCE: put after a date, BCE stands for Before Common Era and counts down to zero. CE stands for Common Era and counts up from zero. These nonreligious terms correspond to BC and AD. This book was printed in 2017 CE.

biodegradable: anything that can be decomposed by organisms.

biophysicist: someone who studies how physical laws affect living things.

ceremony: an event to celebrate or honor something, such as a god or a holiday.

chaos: complete disorder.

citizenship: legally belonging to a country and having the rights and protection of that country.

civil engineering: the branch of engineering that deals with the design, construction, and maintenance of public projects such as bridges, tunnels, and roads, and public buildings or spaces.

civilization: a complex form of culture that includes cities, specialized workers, government and religious institutions, and advanced technology.

Glossary

coding: using a computer-based language to write or build programs.

collaboration: working together with someone else.

colleague: a person with whom one works.

columns: pillars that hold up part of a building.

commercial: relating to the buying and selling of goods or services, with the purpose of making money.

compass: a tool used by architects to draw circles or arcs.

complex: complicated.

consultant: someone who provides advice professionally.

contemporary: modern, existing now, belonging to the current moment.

contractor: a person or company that undertakes a contract to provide materials or labor to perform a service or do a job.

coveted: something that is desired by many people.

conviction: a firmly held belief.

culture: the beliefs and way of life of a group of people, which can include religion, language, art, clothing, food, holidays, and more.

dedication: in architecture, a ceremony for a building once it is completed.

design: planning how a building or other object, such as clothing, will look before it is built.

developer: in architecture and real estate, those who buy, renovate, and sell or rent properties.

dictation: saying words aloud to be typed or written down.

discrimination: the unjust treatment of some groups of people based on their race, religion, or sex.

disparity: a big difference; inequality.

distinctive: unique in appearance or function.

distort: to change or to give a misleading account of something.

diversity: a range of different people or things.

drafting: to draw or sketch out in architecture.

durable: something that lasts for a long time.

elements: the weather and other aspects of nature.

embark: to begin something.

endocrinologist: a medical doctor who treats the endocrine system of the body (the pancreas, thyroid gland, and other glands) and its diseases.

energy efficient: something that reduces the total amount of energy used.

engineer: someone who uses science and math to design and build structures such as buildings, bridges, and tunnels.

engineering: the use of science and math in the design and construction of things.

engrave: to cut or carve into a hard surface.

entomologist: a scientist who studies insects.

environment: the area in which something lives.

equitable: fair and equal.

estimate: to roughly calculate or a rough calculation.

excel: to be very good at a particular activity.

expertise: skill or knowledge in a particular area.

extracurricular: activities pursued outside of study.

force: a push or pull applied to an object.

formative: something that has had a profound and lasting affect on someone.

formwork: molds typically made of wood into which concrete is poured during construction.

foundation: the underlying base of something.

functional: practical and useful.

golden mean: the division of a line so that the ratio between the whole to the larger section is the same as the larger section to the smaller section. This proportion was thought of by the Greeks as being the most beautiful.

Gothic: a style of architecture used in Europe from the twelfth through sixteenth centuries.

gravity: a force that pulls all objects to the earth.

Greek Revival: a style of architecture that incorporates Greek influences that was popular in the early nineteenth century.

harmony: peace and agreement.

hearth: an area in a house where fire was made for heat and cooking.

human resources: the people of a business or organization.

hunter-gatherer: a person who hunts or gathers their food.

iconic: something that is characteristic of an icon, an emblem, or a hero.

immerse: to become absorbed by something.

infinite: limitless or endless, and impossible to measure or calculate.

Glossary

influential: having a strong effect on another person.

innovative: new and creative ideas or methods.

intangible: something that is not physical.

intern architect: an architect who has not yet passed their licensing exams.

intuition: an instinctual feeling rather than rational thought.

licensed: having passed the necessary requirements to participate in a certain field, such as architecture.

linear perspective: a perspective used by architects that involves imagining all lines coming together at a point on the horizon.

load: an applied force or weight.

marvels: wonderful people or things.

mechanical engineering: an area of engineering that deals with the design and construction of machines.

mentor: a more experienced person who guides a younger or more inexperienced person.

milestone: a moment or event that marks an important change.

minority: a group of people, such as African Americans, that is smaller than or different from the larger group.

model: a three-dimensional representation of a person, thing, or proposed structure, typically on a smaller scale than the original.

Modernism: a style of architecture in the twentieth century that focused on simple design and the function of buildings.

nomadic: moving from place to place to find food.

organic architecture: a philosophy of architecture that promotes harmony between humans and the natural world.

organism: a living thing.

ornamentation: in architecture, decoration used to embellish a building.

ornate: a building, for example, that has many intricate designs.

orthogonals: parallel lines drawn diagonally, used in the technique of linear perspective.

paleontologist: a scientist who studies fossils.

Palladian movement: a European style of architecture established by the architect Andrew Palladio in the sixteenth century.

perpendicular: when an object forms a right angle with another object.

perspective: drawing objects on paper so that they appear properly sized in relation to one another.

pharaoh: a ruler of ancient Egypt.

pharmaceutical: anything that relates to medical drugs.

physics: the study of physical forces, including matter, energy, and motion, and how these forces interact with each other.

plane: a flat surface.

predator: an animal that eats other animals by hunting them.

preservation: to keep something protected for future generations.

principal: in architecture, the owner of a firm.

product designer: someone who creates and designs new products.

proportion: a part that is compared in relation to the whole.

proposal: a plan that is presented to others.

proprietary: relating to an owner or ownership.

pulley: a wheel through which a cord passes, used to lift heavy objects.

pyramid: a monument in the shape of a triangle with a square base.

recruit: to enlist or enroll someone to do something.

Renaissance: a cultural movement or "rebirth" that took place in Europe from the fourteenth through the seventeenth centuries.

representation: the description or portrayal of a person or thing.

right angle: the intersection of two perpendicular lines.

Roman Empire: the large empire centered in Rome, in present-day Italy, that was founded in 753 BCE, according to legend.

schematic design: a beginning design in architecture that plans out the general scope of a project, largely without details.

scholarship: funds that are used to pay for a student's education, usually based on a student's academic merit.

science: the study of the physical and natural world.

settlement: a place where a group of people moves to start a new community.

skyscraper: a very tall building that appears to touch the sky.

Glossary

slide ruler: a ruler with a sliding strip that is used to make calculations.

society: an organized community of people with shared laws, traditions, and values.

spatial composition: using available space to create an image or other composition.

specialization: becoming an expert in a particular subject.

species: a group of living things that are closely related and produce young.

spiritual: religious.

stability: the ability of an object to maintain a certain position without collapsing.

stress: pressure or tension.

structural engineering: a kind of civil engineering that focuses on building large structures.

structure: something that is built, such as a building, bridge, tunnel, tower, or dam.

sustainable: something that is able to be used without being completely used up.

symbol: an image or character that stands for something else.

symmetrical: a property of a shape that looks the same if you rotate it or look at it in a mirror.

technology: the use of science to invent needed things or to solve problems.

temple: a building in which people worship gods and practice religious observances.

tenacity: persistence or determination.

thesis: a long essay or paper involving research, usually required for graduation from an academic program.

tracing paper: a transparent paper used by architects to trace and transfer drawings and designs.

transformation: a dramatic or extreme change.

treatise: a philosophical or scientific exploration in writing of a particular subject.

tsunami: a very large ocean wave, usually caused by an earthquake.

tutor: a private teacher.

urban planning: planning for the development of cities and large towns.

vanishing point: a point on the horizon line used in linear perspective through which all parallel lines (orthogonals) meet.

work ethic: a set of values that promotes hard work.

Resources

Books

- *The Future Architect's Handbook*. Beck, Barbara. Schiffer, Atglen, Pennsylvania, 2014.
- *The Story of Buildings: From the Pyramids to the Sydney Opera House and Beyond*. Dillon, Patrick and Stephen Biesty. Candlewick Press, Somerville, Massachusetts, 2014.
- *Maya Lin: Artist-Architect of Light and Lines*. Harvey, Jeanne Walker and Dow Phumiruk. Henry Holt and Company, New York, 2017.
- *Julia Morgan Built a Castle*. Mannis, Celeste and Miles Hyman. Viking Juvenile, New York, 2006.
- *The World is Not a Rectangle: A Portrait of Architect Zaha Hadid*. Winter, Jeanette. Beach Lane Books, San Diego, California, 2017.

Websites and Museums

- American Institute of Architects (AIA): *aia.org*
- ArchDaily: Women in Architecture: *archdaily.com/tag/women-in-architecture*
- Equity By Design: *eqxdesign.com*
- International Archive of Women in Architecture (IAWA): *spec.lib.vt.edu/IAWA*

QR Code Glossary

- page 3: donsmaps.com/dolnivi.html
- page 11: mathsisfun.com/numbers/golden-ratio.html
- page 17: encyclopedia.kids.net.au/page/ar/Architectural_style
- page 22: fallingwater.org
- page 43: lowesforpros.com/articles/how-5-women-have-found-success-in-the-construction-industry_a1476.html
- page 46: youtube.com/watch?v=lykWgAC3XTc
- page 59: arcspace.com/features/zaha-hadid-architects
- page 68: aia.org/resources/24301-equity-diversity-and-inclusion
- page 77: artsbeat.blogs.nytimes.com/2013/06/14/no-pritzker-prize-for-denise-scott-brown
- page 87: archdaily.com/793858/how-to-succeed-as-a-young-architecture-professor-without-dying-in-the-process

Index

Index